My Info

- Name →
- Mobile →
- Email →
- Facebook →
- Instagram →

Find 50 bucket list ideas at the end of this book

belongs to

_____ & _____

Date of our first meeting:

_____

don't QUIT

My Bucket List

Done?

My Bucket List

Done ?

N° .... ○
N° .... ○
N° .... ○
N° .... ○
N° .... ○
N° .... ○
N° .... ○
N° .... ○
N° .... ○
N° .... ○
N° .... ○
N° .... ○
N° .... ○
N° .... ○
N° .... ○

Title: ....
....

The reason why we want to do this: ....
....

What we need: ....
....

Yes! We did it :)

Date Completed: .... *Location:* ....

The Story: ....
....
....
....

Best part: ....
....

We Learned: ....
....

Do it again? → ○ Yes ○ No

Title:
....
....

The reason why we want to do this: ....
....

What we need: ....
....

Yes! We did it :)

Date Completed: ....   **Location:** ....

☀ **The Story:** ....
....
....
....

◉ **Best part:** ....
....

☀ **We Learned:** ....
....

•••• **Do it again?** ⟶ ◯ Yes ◯ No ••••

Title: ....
....

The reason why we want to do this: ....
....

What we need: ....
....

Yes! We did it :)

Date Completed: .... Location: ....

☀ The Story: ....
....
....
....

◎ Best part: ....
....

☀ We Learned: ....
....

···· Do it again? :⫶⟶ ○ Yes ○ No ····

04

Title: ....

The reason why we want to do this: ....

....

What we need: ....

....

Yes! We did it :)

Date Completed: .... **Location:** ....

The Story: ....

....

....

....

Best part: ....

....

We Learned: ....

....

Do it again? ⟶ ○ Yes ○ No

Title: ....
....

The reason why we want to do this: ....
....

What we need: ....
....

Yes! We did it :)

Date Completed: .... Location: ....

☀ The Story: ....
....
....
....

◎ Best part: ....
....

☀ We Learned: ....
....

••• Do it again? ⟶ ○ Yes ○ No •••

Title: ....
....

The reason why we want to do this: ....
....

What we need: ....
....

Yes! We did it :)

Date Completed: .... Location: ....

☀ The Story: ....
....
....
....

◎ Best part: ....
....

☀ We Learned: ....
....

Do it again? ⟶ ○ Yes ○ No

Title:

The reason why we want to do this:

What we need:

Yes! We did it :)

Date Completed: **Location:**

The Story:

Best part:

We Learned:

Do it again? ○ Yes ○ No

08

Title: ....
....

The reason why we want to do this: ....
....

What we need: ....
....

Yes! We did it :)

Date Completed: .... **Location:** ....

The Story: ....
....
....
....

Best part: ....
....

We Learned: ....
....

Do it again? ⟶ ○ Yes ○ No

Title: ....
....

The reason why we want to do this: ....
....

What we need: ....
....

Yes! We did it :)

Date Completed: .... Location: ....

☀ The Story: ....
....
....
....

◎ Best part: ....
....

☀ We Learned: ....
....

•••• Do it again? ➡ ○ Yes   ○ No ••••

Title: ....
....

The reason why we want to do this: ....
....

What we need: ....
....

Yes! We did it :)

Date Completed: .... Location: ....

☀ The Story: ....
....
....
....

◎ Best part: ....
....

☀ We Learned: ....
....

Do it again? ➝ ○ Yes ○ No

11

Title: ....
....

The reason why we want to do this: ....
....

What we need: ....
....

Yes! We did it :)

Date Completed: .... **Location:** ....

The Story: ....
....
....
....

Best part: ....
....

We Learned: ....
....

Do it again? → ○ Yes ○ No

Title:

The reason why we want to do this:

What we need:

Yes! We did it :)

Date Completed: **Location:**

The Story:

Best part:

We Learned:

Do it again? ○ Yes ○ No

13

Title: ....
....

The reason why we want to do this: ....
....

What we need: ....
....

Yes! We did it :)

Date Completed: .... **Location:** ....

The Story: ....
....
....
....

Best part: ....
....

We Learned: ....
....

Do it again? → ◯ Yes ◯ No

Title: ....
....

The reason why we want to do this: ....
....

What we need: ....
....

Yes! We did it :)

Date Completed: .... Location: ....

☀ The Story: ....
....
....
....

◎ Best part: ....
....

☀ We Learned: ....
....

•••• Do it again? → ◯ Yes ◯ No ••••

Title: ....
....

The reason why we want to do this: ....
....

What we need: ....
....

Yes! We did it :)

Date Completed: .... Location: ....

☀ The Story: ....
....
....
....

◎ Best part: ....
....

☀ We Learned: ....
....

•••• Do it again? ⟶ ◯ Yes ◯ No ••••

16

Title:

The reason why we want to do this:

What we need:

Yes! We did it :)

Date Completed: **Location:**

The Story:

Best part:

We Learned:

Do it again? → ◯ Yes ◯ No

Title: ....
....

The reason why we want to do this: ....
....

What we need: ....
....

Yes! We did it :)

Date Completed: .... Location: ....

The Story: ....
....
....
....

Best part: ....
....

We Learned: ....
....

Do it again? ⟶ ○ Yes ○ No

Title:
....
....

The reason why we want to do this: ....
....

What we need: ....
....

Yes! We did it :)

Date Completed: .... Location: ....

The Story: ....
....
....
....
....

Best part: ....
....

We Learned: ....
....

Do it again? ⟶ ○ Yes ○ No

Title :

The reason why we want to do this :

What we need :

Yes! We did it :)

Date Completed :   Location :

The Story :

Best part :

We Learned :

Do it again? ○ Yes ○ No

Title :

The reason why we want to do this :

What we need :

Yes! We did it :)

Date Completed : .... Location : ....

☀ The Story :

◎ Best part :

☀ We Learned :

Do it again? ○ Yes ○ No

Title :
....
....

The reason why we want to do this : ....
....

What we need : ....
....

Yes! We did it :)

Date Completed : .... Location : ....

The Story : ....
....
....
....
....

Best part : ....
....

We Learned : ....
....

Do it again? ⟶ ◯ Yes ◯ No

22

Title:

The reason why we want to do this:

What we need:

Yes! We did it :)

Date Completed: **Location:**

The Story:

Best part:

We Learned:

Do it again? ○ Yes ○ No

Title: ....
....

The reason why we want to do this : ....
....

What we need : ....
....

Yes! We did it :)

Date Completed : .... Location : ....

☀ The Story : ....
....
....
....

◎ Best part : ....
....

☀ We Learned : ....
....

•••• Do it again? ⟶ ○ Yes ○ No ••••

Title: ....
....

The reason why we want to do this: ....
....

What we need: ....
....

Yes! We did it :)

Date Completed: .... Location: ....

☀ The Story: ....
....
....
....

◎ Best part: ....
....

☀ We Learned: ....
....

Do it again? ⟶ ○ Yes ○ No

Title :

The reason why we want to do this :

What we need :

Yes! We did it :)

Date Completed : .... **Location :** ....

The Story :

Best part :

We Learned :

Do it again? → ◯ Yes ◯ No

Title: ....

The reason why we want to do this: ....

What we need: ....

Yes! We did it :)

Date Completed: .... Location: ....

☀ The Story: ....

◎ Best part: ....

☀ We Learned: ....

Do it again? → ○ Yes ○ No

Title: ....
....

The reason why we want to do this: ....
....

What we need: ....
....

Yes! We did it :)

Date Completed: ....   Location: ....

The Story: ....
....
....
....

Best part: ....
....

We Learned: ....
....

Do it again? ⟶ ◯ Yes ◯ No

Title: ....
....

The reason why we want to do this: ....
....

What we need: ....
....

Yes! We did it :)

Date Completed: .... Location: ....

☀ The Story: ....
....
....
....

◎ Best part: ....
....

☀ We Learned: ....
....

Do it again? ⟶ ◯ Yes ◯ No

Title: ....
....

The reason why we want to do this: ....
....

What we need: ....
....

Yes! We did it :)

Date Completed: .... Location: ....

☀ The Story: ....
....
....
....

◎ Best part: ....
....

☀ We Learned: ....
....

Do it again? → ○ Yes ○ No

Title: ....
....

The reason why we want to do this: ....
....

What we need: ....
....

Yes! We did it :)

Date Completed: .... Location: ....

☀ The Story: ....
....
....
....

◎ Best part: ....
....

☀ We Learned: ....
....

•••• Do it again? :◦⇒→ ◯ Yes ◯ No ••••

Dreams don't work unless you do

50 Bucket List Ideas

1. Dine in an underwater restaurant
2. Rent a glass igloo in Finland to sleep under the northern lights
3. Eat a meal cooked by a celebrity chef
4. Get tattoos togethers
5. Spend a day at a spa and have a couple's massage
6. Go on a safari in Africa
7. Try a winter sport : skiing, snowboarding, skating, etc.
8. Plan a surprise trip for each other
9. Go camping together
10. Get married
11. Dance on the beach at sunset
12. RV across a country
13. Ride camels across a desert
14. Attend a wine tasting
15. Start a side business
16. Sponsor a child
17. Give money anonymously to a stranger
18. See Circle Du Soleil
19. Try role-playing
20. Sing in public together
21. Dive in a submarine and see the Titanic
22. Spend the night at the ice hotel in Quebec
23. Experience 24 hours of daylight in Alaska
24. Have a baby
25. Visit the Haiku Stairs in Oahu, Hawaii

50 Bucket List Ideas

26. Spend Christmas in Aspen
27. Swim in every ocean
28. Hike the Grand Canyon
29. Go backpacking through Europe
30. Get VIP passes to a show/concert
31. Learn new instrument
32. Become financially independent
33. Learn ballroom or salsa dancing together
34. Go to Disneyland
35. Ride in a private jet
36. Go sailing
37. Swim with dolphins or sharks
38. Add a lock to the love lock bridge in Paris
39. Ride a horse on the beach
40. Buy a home
41. Rent a beach house for a week
42. Go scuba diving
43. Go to drive in movie
44. Take a road trip
45. Pay for a stranger's groceries or dinner at a restaurant
46. Say yes to everything for a day
47. Go whale watching
48. Visit all the continents in the world
49. Make a wish at the Trevi Fountain in Rome
50. Host a couple's game night or family game night

www.ingramcontent.com/pod-product-compliance
Lightning Source LLC
Chambersburg PA
CBHW071913070526
44583CB00016B/1976